Advance Comments on *My Thoughts Prefer Side Streets*

"They say angels can fly because they take themselves lightly. This book is full of whimsy and wisdom and will help you take yourself and life, both more seriously and lightly. Here's hoping it helps you fly one of these days."

— *Bill O'Hanlon, psychotherapist, trainer, speaker, coach, and author of 34 books, including* Do One Thing Different

"Leslie Miklosy has done it again: enter another collection of aphoristic sayings and gems of miniature essays. Generous and smart, the essays all address some specific but perennially relevant philosophical or existential issue. The short aphorisms are crystallized versions of the essays: tiny shards that glimmer memorably."

— *Timea K. Szell, senior lecturer in English and director of creative writing, Barnard College, New York*

"Leslie Miklosy's *My Thoughts Prefer Side Streets* can make you laugh and then think…or think and then laugh. In either order, both exercises are beneficial."

— *Gene Perret, comedy writer/teacher, Emmy Award winner, Bob Hope head writer, author of* The New Comedy Writing Step by Step

"On the side streets on which you will travel reading this entertaining and dynamic little book, you will encounter wisdom, common sense, humor, practical philosophy, and a refreshed way to look at life that will surely help and guide you over some potholes when you return to the main street of your own existence."

— *Bill Boggs, TV host, author of* Got What It Takes?: Successful People Reveal How They Made It to the Top—So You Can, Too!

"Leslie Miklosy has the admirable gift of speaking from the center of an intelligence richly informed by broad cultural and professional experience. His thoughts are fresh and to the point. Most important: to read and ponder them is certain to lead to one's own reflection on matters of the heart."

— *James P. Carse, professor emeritus of religion, NYU, author of* Breakfast at the Victory: The Mysticism of Ordinary Experience

"In *My Thoughts Prefer Side Streets* Leslie Miklosy detours from the Information Superhighway to find down-home neighborhoods of thinking. By grappling with problems of living, with integrity, he has opened our collective mindscape to billboards and signposts of the neighborhoods in which we really live. More contemporary than Ben Franklin or Mark Twain, Miklosy's nuggets of wisdom share their timeless quintessence in this little book."

— *Stephen Larsen, psychology professor emeritus, SUNY, author with wife Robin Larsen of* A Fire in the Mind: The Life of Joseph Campbell

"Leslie Miklosy writes about daily life with humor, wisdom and optimism. His book arrived on a morning when I was thinking about my life in real time. I suspect it will arrive in the same way to your house. Wonderful synchronicity!"

— *Gioia Timpanelli, considered one of world's foremost storytellers and "Dean of American Storytelling," author of* What Makes a Child Lucky

"My *Thoughts Prefer Side Streets* is like a mental vitamin, it made me feel good to read it."

— *Gil Cates, founder/producing director of the Geffen Playhouse, Los Angeles, 14-time producer of the annual Academy Awards show*

"Leslie Miklosy's inference is that you can reflect on the past and you can attempt to plan for the future, but you must and need to enjoy the moment. It certainly is not difficult to enjoy this fascinating and unusual look at our day-to-day existence by someone who has lived around the country and around the world."

— *Alvin M. Howe, career military officer and local census office manager, 2010 census*

MY THOUGHTS PREFER SIDE STREETS

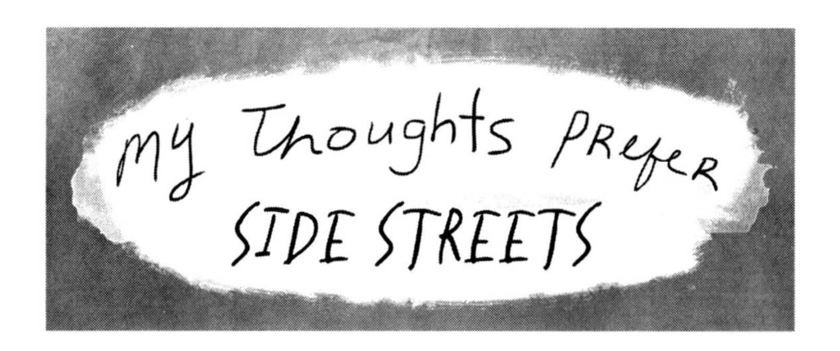

Collected Essays and Other Reflections

Leslie Miklosy

College Station, Texas

"My Thoughts Prefer Side Streets - Collected Essays and Other Reflections," by Leslie Miklosy. ISBN 978-1-60264-899-9.

Published 2011 by Virtualbookworm.com Publishing Inc., P.O. Box 9949, College Station, TX 77842, US.

Manufactured in the United States of America.

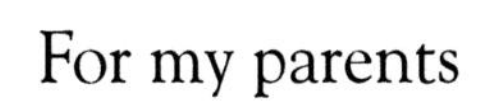
For my parents

Contents

"If I feel physically as if the top of my head
were taken off, I know that is poetry."

– Emily Dickinson
(1830 – 1886)

Preface

Having arrived at middle-age and seeing how far I've traveled, I can't help but ruminate about "what it all means." This compilation of 11 essays, 82 short sayings, and one poem expresses – in ways often unusual, quirky, offbeat – much of what I've come up with so far.

The short sayings – new, original midlife reflections of the sort found in my first book, *Which Is More Round, the World or Your Tummy?: Offbeat Reflections on Serious Living* – are interspersed among the essays. The sayings are quick reads, but sometimes require, and are worth, a thoughtful pause.

The essays aim to be inspirational. All but one of them originally appeared in *The Fayetteville Observer* (Fayetteville, North Carolina's daily newspaper); the essay "My Daily To-do List" came out in *SmartNews* (community periodical no longer in print).

I end with a poem, "Heart to Open," in the Afterword that began as a submission to a Christmas story annual contest – a composition that looked more like a poem than a story, and I reshaped it thus.

My thanks to Catherine Brown, for her lovely book cover artwork; Jack Wilson, for his uniquely inspired drawings; Juan Llanos, for his masterly layout; the industrious folks at VBW Publishing for helping give birth to this book; family and friends for their support and encouragement.

Thanks also to *The Fayetteville Observer* for their permission to reprint the essays.

SMACK
Beginning
The End
is
Near
T. Wilson

CHAPTER 1

Today Is the Happiest Day of My Life

I wake up today with a big smile on my face. Why? Because today is the happiest day of my life. Why is it the happiest day of my life? Because it's a brand new day and I get to start all over again. The sun is shining, the earth sparkles. Birds are singing me a song. The weather, hot or cold, has adjusted and been set, incredibly, just for me to be fine with it.

My to-do list tells me it's going to be an engaging day – a productive day. My aches and pains – and I do have aches and pains – remind me I'm still alive (God bless!). The motor in my brain is cranking up, my place set at the table of life. I will be doing things. I will be going places. I will be talking (maybe even laughing) with people. I will be having new experiences, learning new lessons, building fresh memories. Any corrections needed from yesterday, I'll get to fix those, too. The day will unfold in tandem with my participation. We'll get through it, the day and I, holding hands, getting things done. And if I play my cards right, I'll do it having a rip-roaring good time!

And what about the troubles in the world? Those horrible news events way too huge, way beyond me, way overwhelming? Well, I will do my part, little or large as it may be, consequential or inconsequential in the Great Scheme of Things. The rest is up to God. And what about my own problems? What about my own travails? They will get their due. And they will also remind me that in spite of heaviness and sadness and sickness and pain, the world is my friend.

So, hello friend! I step out of bed, and I begin my wonderful day. And tomorrow? What about tomorrow, you ask? Well, don't even get me started about tomorrow…

The world is, besides so many other things,
A wish-fulfilling machine.
You just have to align with
That aspect of its nature.

A smile at its peak is a very sexy thing.

You can earn your bed & board
By making the world your home.

Every day has its own cereal box prize.

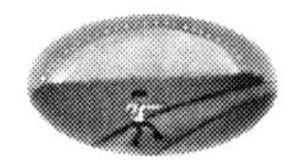

Life consists of the accumulation
Of how we respond to each moment;
And how we respond to each moment
Is at least partly determined
By what each moment brings us;
And to the extent each moment brings us
Something new, or unexpected, or from outside ourselves –
To that extent, life is an adventure.

Silence, space, and time
Are the wrappings
Of great gifts.

Life
Can Be
Great Fun!
T Wilson

CHAPTER 2

Don't Let Opportunity Slip by – Live with Gusto

While there's everything to be said for living a life of integrity and goodness, balance and moderation, service and love – here I want to talk about life as celebration.

Each of us is born equipped for pleasure, for enjoyment. That's basic design, no argument. The news flash, folks, is that sensuality – the art of enjoying the pleasures of the senses – is not only a good thing, it's a very good thing. We can embody both correctness and *joie de vivre*. As we carry out the duties of the day, we can have fun with sight, sound, smell, taste and touch. There's a whole array of possibilities for living with pleasurable appreciation.

Don't let those opportunities slip by. Regret, I'm here to tell you, is one mangy, ill-tempered dog that's best kept outdoors.

How many of us are able to live fully, enriching our days with satisfying experiences, accumulating warm memories that will keep through the winter of our lives? We all can pull from our pasts those special events once embraced and wonderfully absorbed, then permanently recorded for future delightful replay. Who has not taken deep pleasure from a sound snooze, a sumptuous meal, an especially memorable interpersonal romp?

For those who believe in an eternal existence, life can be viewed as a dress rehearsal for the hereafter. Are we proving our worthiness by being open to life's pleasures? Are we able to recognize that life is many things, but also succulent, and draw from its juice? Do we know how to enjoy and have fun? (And for those who believe this is all there is: Get it while you can!). Anyone can be miserable – there's no talent in that. Anyone can live a dull and unimaginative life.

Whether proactively or by opportunity, our task – should we choose to accept it – is to live with gusto. As we proceed through life, let us do so with playful deliberation, with a twinkle in our eyes and a bounce in our steps. We need to relish the moments we've been given. Are we up to the challenge?

Sensuality and art have diversionary value –
They are both engaging and freeing.

What's your life's decibel?

If one is dissatisfied in life,
It's another way of saying
One is blind to opportunities and possibilities.

Without engagement, there can be no marriage.

Tailor-made failure: Living life close-to-the-vest.

Doorknobs can be painful
When not used to open doors.

CHAPTER 3

Would You Like to Come Out and Play?

I have a confession to make: I'm a middle-aged fellow who likes to play. I will, for instance, while in the throes of a particular mood, pretend to lunge at our family dog. The dog – smart animal that he is – picks up on the counterfeit attack and off we go, enjoying our merry little dance.

Or maybe I'll get into a verbal joust with a co-worker. Each of us will try to outdo and outwit the other. With a good repartee started, the rejoinders fly back and forth like Ping-Pong balls, to our mutual delight.

In many situations throughout the day, I'll have occasion to meander, and duck, and twist and turn, bop and weave, turn inside out and stop on a dime.

There are infinite ways of expressing play. It can be its own activity, or it can simply be imbued in a context to make it "playful."

There is solitary play (with or without imaginary friends) and communal play. You can break into song, do a little Irish jig or make faces in the mirror.

If you feel like it, you can have long, absurd conversations with yourself (wearing a phone earpiece in public, for the sanity police). With family, friends and foils, you can enact wondrous scenarios that cover the range of human experience – putting your own peculiar spin on them.

What is it about play that is so satisfying? Well, it's fun, it's creative, and it breaks – temporarily – those confining boundaries of serious reality.

Play uplifts and exercises; it regulates and displaces; it modifies and modulates. You can understate with it or exaggerate. You can explode a moment with a quip or go off on a long riff.

Play is about possibilities. It can contain – among other things – humor, surprise, mystery, whimsy and extravagance.

Play doesn't need research, doesn't need to be proven. It requires no down payment. It fits into small spaces, wears well and is highly portable. And it contains no calories.

Serious business needs to be taken seriously, of course, but a pause here and there – a little playing here and there – will take the enterprise of living further and farther, while keeping it from going afield. So let yourself be light of foot and spirit.

Next time there's a knock on your door, and the tooth fairy, or Santa Claus, or the Jolly Green Giant says to you, "Can Mr. Silly come out and play?" be smart and say "Yes!"

What if
On the seventh day,
God did not say,
"Let us rest,"
But rather,
"Let us play"?

Oxymoron: Meaning what?

He's become quite good at going out
And walking his doggone it!

If I had more time to hurry,
I could relax faster.

The thrust of the story
Generated a pregnant pause.

The raconteur regaled us
With tales of raccoons in Rangoon.

I dance to the song
Within and between
The words.

Stage fright: Hamstrung.

Amoral: Playing musical chairs with your virtues and vices.

1)
2)
3)

CHAPTER 4

My Daily To-do List

I hate to-do lists. It's not that I'm undisciplined or can't get things done. I just prefer a looser style. Everything needing my attention gets its time and place. Items small or large, pressing or not, at the top of the list or down – I juggle and spin them in my own uniquely creative way, sometimes following the rules of good time management and sometimes not. My way works for me and I'm satisfied with it.

There is one category of tasks, however, that does lend itself to the restraints of a to-do list: the life-defining, big picture activities outside the parameters of mundane living. Here are a few for consideration:

1. *Give more than you receive.* One of the secrets of life is that the more you give, the more you have with which to give, and therefore the more you have.

2. *Admire the beauty in the world.* All around us – if we are attentive – can be found the boundless richness of creation. Just open yourself up to it and see how quickly you'll feel better.

3. *Tell your loved ones that you love them.* When you exercise love, you live in love. What can be better than that?

4. *Practice gratitude.* The good in your life needs your acknowledgment, at the very least to underscore your worthiness for more good to come your way.

5. *Be productive.* Not only does it boost your spirit, but it also increases your resources. It gives power, and brings freedom. It's an all-purpose tonic with no side effects.

6. *Challenge yourself in some way.* The momentum of life dictates that you either grow or decline. Be a righteous warrior. Beat back your fears and watch your world expand.

7. *Exercise personal qualities important to you.* Whether you'd like to be kinder, or wiser, or more confident – the best way to embody a trait is to practice it. The more you do something, the more you incorporate it.

It's easy to neglect what needs doing. Life presents us with so many distractions every day disguised as obligations and opportunities that we can miss what is most important. A list can make the difference between living well and living poorly.

Let's see, what do I need to do today?

Exercise effortlessness.

Some people are too good
At trying too hard
To be too happy.

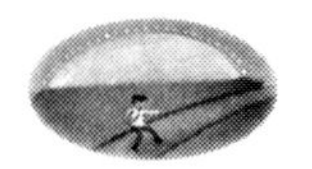

An exercise:
Each day build up a scenario,
In great detail,
Of another way of life.
A different one each day.

Don’t ever let one moment
Take anything away
From another.

If you're looking for family,
Cry "Uncle."

Don't spill the now.

CHAPTER 5

Take the Invite to Be Generous

Years ago, while living in New York City, I was approached by a panhandler at the subway station while on my way to work. I reached into my pocket and gave the man a quarter. He looked at what I had given him and – to my great dismay – began shouting at me, berating me for how little it was. If I'd had a hat, I would have pushed it up on my forehead in amazement as I pondered the fact that I was the only person, as far as I could see, to give the man anything – yet I had been singled out for his very public displeasure.

Another time, also in New York, during a brutal winter evening, I bought a hot soup and gave it to another homeless man who was shivering in the cold. With deep appreciation, he blessed me and my future offspring for my small kindness.

I haven't always responded to the destitute when they have crossed my path. And I can't explain why sometimes I have, and sometimes I haven't. Probably it was a confluence of my state of mind and the particular circumstance. I can remember being asked for help immediately after some good fortune had befallen me, and giving out of a sense of not wanting to tempt the fates with a lack of generosity. Other times, while in a bad mood, I've firmly but politely told the person looking for a handout that, sorry, I can't help you. And the truth is that while some of those times I really couldn't, at other times I just wanted to be left alone and not bothered.

Panhandlers actually are a very special group of people who live among us. They are like us – young and old, male and female, all racial types and cultures. What makes them unique, even apart from their unfortunate station in life, is the fact that they spend their days "inviting" members of the community to exercise a sense of generosity.

What they do is give us the opportunity – at that particular moment in time – to be the best of who we are, of who we can be. And like a filter, they engage those who accept that spiritual invitation while pushing away those others who would rather not. So, in a manner of speaking, they can be said to spend their days visiting with the finest members of our larger human family – just from being who they are and doing what they do.

Who are these magnets of goodness? They are known by many names: panhandlers, the destitute, poor people, marginal folk, the indigent, vagrants, bums, street people, beggars, scam artists, life's unfortunates, tramps. Their journeys to their current situations are as individual and varied as they are. Some never had a chance; some had great awful luck; some chose badly. Their public faces also are diverse – from the seemingly normal to the mentally ill; from the shabby but dignified to the filthy; from the innocuously modest to the obnoxiously aggressive.

On the road of life, when our business and their business occasionally meet, we can and do respond in many ways. Our challenge, if we think about it, is who will we be at that moment of interaction, of invitation, of opportunity. Will we be our most generous self? Our most impatient self? Our feeling-guilty self? Our self-righteous self? Our play-it-safe self? Our benefit-of-the-doubt self? Our won't-be-cheated self? Our there-but-for-the-grace-of-God self?

Bottom line, we can empathize with the struggles of a fellow human being and respond from our heart. Or we can groan at the approach of an outstretched hand or the beginning of an involved sad story. We can – and do – find reasons not to encourage their expressions of need, or neediness (and do we differentiate between, and respond selectively to, seeming actual need versus seeming neediness?).

I would submit that during these moments of "invitation," the larger questions of whether we should support such relationships of dependence, or possible fraud, are less important than what we are called to do at that moment and how we respond. Life is, after all, an accumulation of moments. Each moment can be seen as a test, and as an opportunity. An opportunity to express who we are. An opportunity to become who we want to be.

So who would I like to be?

Too much of not enough.

Yearnings of an outsider: A place in the sum.

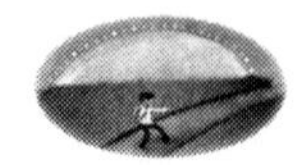

Some people max out their credit cards;
Others, their needs.

Time to give notice,
Or time to notice and give?

One can only receive by giving.
One can only survive by receiving.
So reach in your pocket…and live.

If someone wants to give you something,
You shouldn't take that away from them.

Welcome to Life!

CHAPTER 6

Wisdom Means Doing the Best We Can

We as human beings are attracted to the good and repulsed by the bad. This is the basic impulse of life, and there is wisdom in it. There is, however, also subtlety in life – and that is the difference between what is good and what seems good, and what is bad and what seems bad. How we navigate between those two sets of poles determines and defines our lives.

We begin this earthly journey with a certain preparation. For some, many of the tools to construct a worthwhile life are given. For others, the task is more difficult. Their challenge includes figuring out what is needed, figuring out how and where to obtain it, and obtaining it.

The obstacles we encounter in the process of living our lives are tailor-made for us – or so we believe. Each of us must play the cards we are dealt, we are told. God does not give us more hardship than we can handle, is the truism.

What, then, are we given to guide us? How do we know moment-to-moment what direction to take, what choices to make? We are presented with two categories of signs: internal and external.

The internal ones have to do with our intelligence, our thoughts, and our emotions. Our intelligence is the mechanism by which we interpret the thoughts and feelings that present themselves to us. We draw conclusions deliberately from them, or they arrive unannounced and ready-made as intuitions.

The external signs are related to the circumstances of our lives and the manifestations of the world around us. We are players and enactors. We embody, and we act and react. These signs together move us in directions sometimes evident and sometimes mysterious, and result in the panoply of our individual lives.

There are those who would define our place in the world in one of two ways. One is that we are free agents exercising free will; the other is that our responses are, if not pre-determined, predicated entirely and inevitably by the variables of who we are and how life comes at us. It seems, if one looks at it with an open mind, that both ways can be seen as true. And if that is so, then some higher incomprehensible interplay between the two – between determinism and free choice – must hold.

In the final analysis, our understanding – limited as it is – is at best conjecture. (If you don't believe this, just look at the history of mankind's convictions about reality through the ages.) We hypothesize and make pronouncements – often with great emotional investment and sometimes even with violence. But ultimately, if we are to be honest, we are drawn back again and again to an uncomfortable realization: While we think that we do and we hope that we do, we don't really know. And, under those circumstances, the best we can do is...do the best we can.

Your gifts and your interests,
And circumstance,
Are your agenda in life.

When long term plans are coy,
Mix any day's who-you-are
With whatever comes
Into your orbit.

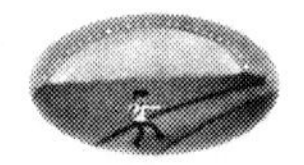

Too much belaboring, not enough laboring.

What byways and back roads
Will lead me to the front of my life?

Everything leads somewhere
And therefore
Can lead you out
Of anywhere.

If I lose my way,
Can I take somebody else's?

REST AREA

CHAPTER 7

Problems and Solutions Made for Each Other

There are problems in life. There are solutions in life. And the funny thing about problems and solutions is that they have a relationship with each other: They seek each other out.

At various times during the course of living, we are presented with one problem or another. (You may hear a voice from above, or from within, say, "Here it is. Now play with it.") Since life is a full-menu experience, those problems may range from minor, annoying ones to overwhelming, impossible ones. They come uninvited, and may stay for a short time or for what seems like forever.

Our task in the face of a problem is simply to engage it. Not deny or ignore it – not run away from it – but to meet it head-on. Be willing and ready to do what we can to try and work it out. Our commitment and effort then become the trumpet call that draws solutions to come-a-courting.

Solutions come in many guises. They are not always initially recognized; they may even show themselves dressed up as other problems. They can make a grand entrance or quietly slip in through a back door. Whatever their appearance or manner of expression, solutions exist to meet up with problems that match them. Problems and solutions gravitate toward each other, join up and ride off together into the sunset.

Unburdened, we are left invigorated, refreshed and renewed. We are strengthened by the exercise of overcoming a challenge. We are prepared once again to be a player in the Great Game of Life.

So next time you're ambushed by a nasty situation, little or large, out of left field – next time you're immersed in a problem, stewing in misery – be assured that resources are available to help you with whatever test life may bring. Don't be resigned or defeated. Be engaged, be a participant. Solutions already exist. And they await their call.

Any movement toward solution gathers energy;
Any movement away from solution depletes energy.
Act accordingly.

Me and the world,
We duke it out
From time to time:
The world wants
What it wants
From me,
And I don't always
Wanna give it.

Misery should make one hopeful –
It implies the existence
Of a correct, happy fit.
And the rest is just travel.

A dead end is the only way out
Of where you shouldn't be going.

Entrenchment is only a problem
While you can still pay its rent.

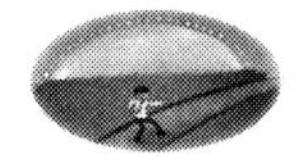

Will my birthright
Turn out to be retroactive?

The insurance would not pay
For the whiplash,
No matter how good the belly dance.

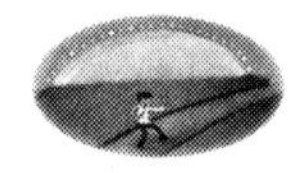

Painmates of long ago
Will do best
To remain unreminding.

Drama.
Sexy from the outside;
Shitty from the inside.

When you fall,
Where you land is where you live.

Midlife crisis: *Mortar* fear.

You are the navigational system
Out of your own conundrum.

CHAPTER 8

We Can Only Do What We Can Do

We have considered that solutions already exist that will solve the problems in our lives. And that they await their call through our attempt to work out those problems. And that once they match up with their corresponding problems, those problems no longer have a hold on us and take their leave.

Does that work in all situations? No, of course not. There are problems, chronic or catastrophic, that have no solution. They are so gigantic and intractable they permanently rearrange the furniture of our lives. They forever alter the landscape of possibilities. If we let them, they can easily crush our spirits.

There's a popular saying that claims we are given in life only as much burden as we can handle, and no more. But a fairly cursory glance all around disproves it. In real life all over the world, people get overwhelmed, are crushed, lose everything. What consolation exists for anyone on such a nightmare journey?

Problems may loom so large that they cast a suffocating shadow on the remainder of our lives. Even so, they are still subservient to the greater expression of all that we are. Problems affect us, and push us, and force us to react – but even in an unwinnable game, we are vital players. We may lose the game, but we don't have to lose ourselves.

Insoluble problems tempt us in several ways: They lead us to believe we no longer control our lives; they convince us we've forfeited all possibilities for a meaningful existence; they invite us to enter despair. We can either give in, or we can toughen up – and endure. And we endure by reaching inside ourselves and using whatever helps us: faith, stubbornness, vanity, fear.

Endurance brings its own rewards. When stripped of strength, we discover a self that doesn't rely on strength. When stripped of identification with who we used to be, we discover our core being (and then find out, truly, who we really are).

When the worst that can happen, happens – what is expected of us? How do we deal with problems of that magnitude? How do we cope when in their grip? The answer may be that when there is no solution, magic or otherwise, we simply endure. We live day-by-difficult-day. We plow forward. Because ultimately, we solve problems we can solve; and we live with – endure – problems we can't solve. We can only do what we can do...but we can do that.

When you're empty, go with empty.

He was host
To a whole lot of trouble.

Not doing swimmingly:
Currently trapped in an undertow,
Awash in problems.

Problem got you in a bear hug?
Wait it out, pal.
Onliest advice I've got.

Moments are like gas, they pass.

The other side of pain and trouble
Is much the same as
The other side of pleasure and happiness,
N'est pas?

The content of each day
Pours out,
Sometimes sunshine,
Sometimes rain.
But the evening's darkness
Covers all the same.

CHAPTER 9

What We Know and What We Don't Know

We know many things about the world we live in. Some of those things are correct; some of them are incorrect. The incorrect ones reside in our informational blind spot – we are not aware they are incorrect. Even greater than what we don't know because we know it in error is the vast information beyond us about which we don't even have a clue.

Although what we don't know about the world eludes us, we have a definite relationship to it. Some of us are afraid of the unknown. Others of us romanticize it. A few of us vigorously pursue it. Most of us are blissfully unmindful of and unconcerned with the entire category. We are content to spend our lives within the confines of what has already been mapped out and defined. And yet all that we know is clearly only a subset of all that exists, and is in affiliation with the rest of that knowledge which we have so far not achieved.

To our credit, we humans throughout history have endeavored to learn – and learn more – about the world around us and even inside us. The paths we have taken in service of that quest have at times been noble, and at times shameful. Knowledge sought to help humanity, to better ourselves, has been a pursuit borne of our best inclinations. Selfish and evil impulses, on the other hand, have led us to search for ways to subjugate and destroy our fellows and our environment.

The unknown is a cache of possibilities that will define our future – the future of mankind. The key to success in our search is the simple rule that the unknown is an extension of the known. Those who resist the unknown deny that rule.

It remains to be seen whether there is an intelligence to how our readiness for new knowledge relates to our acquisition of that knowledge. For some, that question has already been answered, one way or another; for others, it is an intriguing part of the great puzzle of life – a cliffhanger in our journey to tomorrow.

If we are to be wary
Of that which entices,
What, then, is left?

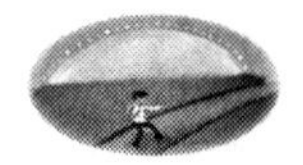

Will you treat
People who make you miserable
As prison guards,
Or travel agents?

How do the things we are against,
Exemplify the nature of existence?
And should we therefore
Be against them?

Belief depends on definition;
Definition is based on limit;
Truth has no limit except itself.
Therefore belief cannot encompass truth –
It can only suggest it.

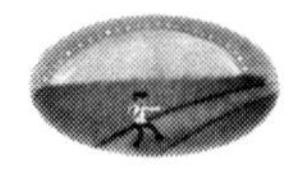

When one is in relationship
With the truth,
It is – fundamentally –
A happy marriage.

Religion is not so much
A vehicle to God,
As it is a buffer
Against the harshness
Of the brilliance
Of the purity
Of God.

CHAPTER 10

My Self and I, for Better or Worse

OK, so here I am in the world, a self among other selves. God only knows how I got here. I am a construction with limited warranty and non-replaceable parts. I am a working model of worldliness, a manifestation of material from parts unknown. And the self that I am, that became what it is from what it started out as – well, I have a few things to say on that subject.

First of all, being me is hard work. As much as I want to, there's no denying it. Whether I asked for it or not, it's a 24-hour-a-day, seven-days-a-week, often grueling, frustrating, confusing job. And there's no sick leave. It's always me – yesterday, today and tomorrow. Me, me, me.

It all can be quite exhausting. I am a full stage production, with many lead actors and hundreds of extras, with expensive sets, and a full range of lights and special effects. Underplaying is not my game. Holding back is just the first step of a full wind-up and let-it-all-out pitch across home plate.

Did I say being me is a tough gig? At times, even practically impossible. Copycats and identity thieves beware, you're wasting your time. You're better off plying your dirty work elsewhere. There is no reward for you in this neck of the woods. My self is no picnic, no day at the beach. And the only satisfaction achievable is inherent, specifically pre-programmed to my DNA, and my DNA only.

There are times I like and agree with myself – as if we were compatible roommates; or inseparable companions. Of course, there are other not infrequent occasions when even my reflection pains me, when the reality and the fantasy of my self-image inhabit not only different worlds, but wholly opposite universes. My voice then joins the chorus of those whose entire purpose in life seems to be to cause me as much misery as is humanly possible. (OK, I exaggerate. There is no conspiracy.)

It's my job to not only define myself, orient myself, nourish myself, and keep motivating myself – but I'm also entrusted with blazing a unique path through this intractable existence and claiming my chunk of worldly selfhood, with all the frills and garnishing that such a presence entails. My entitlement in this life is whatever I can claim through achievement and good fortune. Let the chips fall where they may.

There's no avoiding being me – being me is my passport to living life as a full-fledged human being. The way is not always clear, however. My instruction manual on how to be me did not come with the package. I'm actually having to write the manual as I go along. But given time, authority will come from authorship. And authenticity. I'm working my way through college, as it were.

Whether I can become the self that realizes itself (take that however you wish) remains to be seen. I guess it depends on whether I'm a puzzle or mystery to be solved. Or not.

I only have just one final question: When I pass by a mirror and see myself smiling, am I supposed to smile back?

Entertained and distracted
By life's sideshows,
We master the mundane
And become expert in the irrelevant.

Self enamoredness, a deadly (though not fatal) disease.

When you're young,
Wishes-that-come-true
Are like erasers –
They rub out parts of your self.

Saying “no” to yourself
Can be a way of saying “yes” to yourself.

If you pretend
To be you,
You will inevitably
Be unmasked.

Her make-up was part of her make-up.

If there are many aspects
To who I am,
Which is the last one
To turn out the lights?

I conduit.

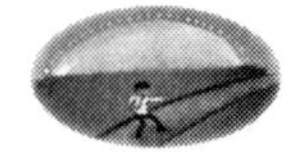

He always had required a lot of space:
When he was born, they found
An umbilical *and* an extension cord.

Do not reduce me to an understanding.
I am more than that.

Who has not gotten lost,
Sometime or other,
In their own subtleties?

Of all things, I had to choose *inner* excellence!

CHAPTER 11

Have Faith While in Life's Grip

We all harbor illusions about living an ideal life. Someday, we think, all our dreams will come true and we will finally be blissfully happy; we will live life our own way. That is, we tell ourselves, our destiny: to meet all our challenges, achieve all our goals, to succeed. Otherwise, what is it all for?

The truth is, as everyone eventually finds out, life has other plans for us. Our agenda and life's agenda for us turn out to be two different things. And that is part of the great mystery of our lives. There are detours that take us in entirely new directions from the ones we expect. We are forced to deal with events we would never have chosen to be involved in. We have experiences we could never have anticipated. And in the end, we become ourselves – we mature into our true selves – through living with and grappling with and overcoming problems that were made to order for us by whatever intelligence orchestrates the universe and our place in it. The delicious irony of it all is that the inevitable self we become is us through and through – yet the process of getting there is beyond our intention, beyond our understanding.

All this is to say that life – not you nor I – is in charge. We are in its grip. We would like to think we are in the driver's seat, but we are not. Whether because of job loss, or incapacitating illness, or myriad other circumstances leaving us feeling helpless and unaware of any possible resolution, we come to the stark knowledge that we are not in control. Is this realization – when we finally achieve it – cause for distress, or even despair? Consider this: If life consisted only of what we hoped and imagined, there would be no room for surprise or excitement or exhilaration. If life was predictable, even in a good way, it would still be dull. Is that a recipe we would want to be part of? I don't believe so.

That is actually our challenge – learning to have faith that there is a purposeful design that directs us as we were meant to be directed; that life's purpose for us is grander than our own poorly-imagined one. In the end – despite the occasional roller coaster rides, the difficult midlands we may have to travel through, the seemingly dead ends – life promises not only to be good but to be great! For, after all, our real destiny is to become ourselves.

While in the desert,
You never hear,
"I'll drink to that!"

If you want to have
A relationship with the world,
You have to accept
That the world
Will sometimes say
"No."

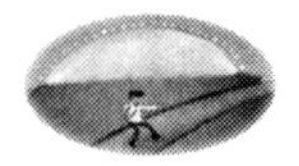

Maybe the things you think you want
Will not get you the things you think
They might have gotten you.

Off the lower end of the scales, my shantytown.

Own your problems,
Own your mistakes,
And you, too,
Can be a real estate magnate.

In time, life shrink wraps
Down to your greatness;
Ragged ideas are tossed
In favor of snug reality;
Self is finally tailor-made.
Tap dance, grasshopper!

Afterword

Heart to Open

When we are born, God gives each of us a heart.
While you live, take care of it, He says.

Like a drum, our heart plays music –
Boom Ba-Boom, Boom Ba-Boom –
Helping us to dance to Life's Sweet Song.

Like a compass, our heart points
From There to Here, from Then to Now.
We carry it around, so we know where and when we are.

Like a soft pillow, our heart helps us feel
The world gently, and press back softly.
When we're tired, it gives us a place to rest.

Most of all, our heart carries Love, a lifetime supply.
Everyone we meet is like a thirsty flower –
Ready to be nourished, ready to bloom.

So open your heart, and share yourself.
A life lived well, congratulations!

About the Author

Leslie Miklosy is an essayist, aphorist, interviewer, poet, and joke writer. He is the author of *Which Is More Round, the World or Your Tummy?: Offbeat Reflections on Serious Living*, a collection of his midlife musings about various aspects of the life journey.

Leslie has lived in Argentina, Venezuela, and in the U.S. mostly in North Carolina and New York. A former administrator in mental health and philanthropy, he currently works as a school teacher.

His longtime interests include storytelling, mythology, psychotherapy, and comedy. He enjoys wordplay and the vain pursuit of answers to life's larger questions.

Leslie can be contacted at lesliebks@hotmail.com

Gasp

Notes

Notes

Notes

Notes